Going to new places

Asking a question in class

Going to parties where you hardly know anyone

Meeting someone for the first time

Everyone feels shy from time to time.

How does shyness make you feel?

We show that we are feeling shy in different ways.

I get tummy ache.

I go hot all over.

4

Shyness can make us feel awkward, and stop us from behaving naturally. It might make it hard for you to look at people when they are talking to you, or when you are trying to reply.

When I feel shy, I can't think of anything to say.

Do you know how you act when you are feeling shy?

It makes me giggle.

It's not wrong to feel shy and you don't need to find a cure. But it will help if you can learn how to cope with it in different situations.

Clare and Janet both feel a bit shy when they meet new people. Janet starts by asking a question.

Have you read this book? It's great!

Janet says, "If I start talking about something interesting, I get really involved after a while. Then I forget I felt shy to begin with."

When I talk to someone, I try to look at their face and smile.

Craig says he finds that most people smile back at him, which makes him feel much better, and not nearly so shy.

If you have something difficult to say, it can make you feel very awkward and shy. Sometimes, it takes a lot of courage to tell your parents or a teacher about something that is worrying you.

When Matt does manage to tell his mum about a problem, she listens to him carefully, and is very helpful.

Mum, I want to tell you something, but I'm scared you'll laugh at me.

Adults don't always listen properly. Try to talk to them at a time when you know they can give you their full attention. Choose a grown-up in your family, a grown-up friend or a teacher that you like.

Do you ever feel shy about saying or doing something different? Perhaps you are worried that other people might laugh at you for it.

Rashida says, "I felt very shy when I told my family I didn't want to eat meat any more. No one else in our house is vegetarian."

"But when I told the others at school how I felt, quite a lot of them agreed with me."

When you say how you feel, you will often find that other people feel the same way.

I think it's wrong to kill animals!

Sometimes, grown-ups can make you feel very shy.

Kate says, "When we go to see Uncle Josh, his family all talk at once and laugh a lot."

They keep asking me questions but they never really listen to what I say!

"Mum says not to worry and that they make her feel shy too. She says that I should write them a thank you letter to show that I do care, even though I'm always so quiet at their parties."

Some people feel shy of singing, acting, or even talking in front of other people. Grown-ups don't always understand why you don't want to join in. They worry that you are not enjoying yourself.

Janek says, "I always hated going to parties, because I felt silly joining in with the games. Now I get out of playing games by helping to organise them instead."

Do some situations make you feel especially awkward? Can you think of any ways to change these situations so that you would feel more comfortable?

Rebecca curled up with embarrassment when her dad came into school one day.

But her friends said their parents made them feel embarrassed or shy at times too. We have to learn to accept that everyone is different. We can't expect our parents to change just so they don't embarrass us.

His clothes are all wrong! Everyone will laugh!

Some people will always say things to tease others. But as you get older, you will find that you don't get so upset by them. Perhaps this is because you don't pay as much attention to them.

The same is true for feeling shy. People don't stop feeling shy, but gradually their shyness becomes easier to manage, and they worry about it less.

At the moment, you may feel that you want to be the same as everyone else. Perhaps you don't want to look different or be different in any way. But you probably want to feel special as well.

As you get older, you might find that it's not so bad being different, and that you like yourself the way you are. Imagine how boring the world would be if we were all the same!

For teachers and parents

A note from Dorothy Rowe

Parents and teachers know that feeling shy is a common problem for children. But they sometimes forget that in order to help, they must first find out how the child sees the problem. A child won't see the situation in the same way as an adult, because no two people ever see things in exactly the same way.

Remembering this, an adult will not assume that they know what is wrong with a child, but will explore alternative possible reasons for the child's shyness. They might ask themselves, 'Is this child shy because she's frightened of other children?', or 'Is she shy because she's had some bad experiences and doesn't want to get hurt again?'. It's possible to think up dozens of alternative answers to the question, 'Why does this child behave in this way?'. Doing so helps the adult to ask better questions. However, the answer can only come from the child.

Feeling shy isn't a problem we can solve once and for all, but a dilemma we have to live with all our lives. To help a child understand this, the adult should not pretend to have solved the problem, but rather be prepared to talk about their own difficulties in dealing with it. This way, the adult and the child can explore the dilemma together. There is no cure for feeling shy; people just have to find ways to cope with their shyness.

To start a discussion, and to get everyone involved, both you and the children could write a list of all the things that make you shy, then compare your lists.

Alternatively, you could compile a list of situations which can cause shyness, and, with the children, write down after each whether they make you feel 'Very Shy', 'A Bit Shy', or 'Not Shy'. Examples might include:

- Walking into a room full of people that you don't know; or having to say goodbye and leave a room full of people.

- Being called into the teacher's office.

- Being insulted by someone.

Compare your answers and be honest. Many adults still feel shy if they have to go and see the head teacher!

Many ideas can be discussed page by page when going through the book again. But the following may prove useful starting points:

Page 5
If you don't look at people when they talk to you, or you talk to them, they may feel it's because you don't like them.

Page 6
It's more important to be friendly than to worry about what you say.

Page 9

People can feel shy in new situations, when they don't know what is going to happen next.

Page 14

It may not only be worries that children are shy of sharing. They may feel shy about telling their parents about something interesting that they have learnt, or something exciting which has happened to them.

Page 15

People may also feel shy of saying how they feel because they think someone might laugh at them.

Page 18/19

Sometimes, adults ask silly questions because they feel shy and don't know how to talk to children. It may be difficult to answer without sounding rude, so the child seems shy too.

Adults sometimes make comments about children within their hearing; that's enough to make anyone feel shy.

Everyone is shy at times. It's not what happens to us, but how we feel about what happens to us that leads to a feeling of shyness.

Further reading

Children may find it interesting and helpful to have a look at some of the following story books, which also deal with the subject of feeling shy.

Mark Haddon
The Real Porky Philips
A & C Black (1995)

Kaye Umansky
Sophie and the Wonderful Picture
Gollancz, Cassell (1995)

Sam McBratney
Art, You're Magic
Walker Sprinters,
Walker Books (1995)

Sally Christie
Not Just Jemima
Walker Books (1992)

E B White
Charlotte's Web
Puffin Books (1996)